Little Black Book

BY: KATIE GUNTER

I dedicate this art to a part of me that will never be okay, but has learned to accept and face my decline into insanity.

Little Black Book: Intro

I gave myself therapy through these pages
marked with lead.

I filled them with sorry stories of the voices
contained in my head.

There's no easing the rattle once the serpent
sees.

The pen is my apple; I write the words of a
deadly disease.

What has been written once, hasn't been
written again.

What's meant to be said, bleeds out in pen.

Poetic confusion is, to me, what those letters
spell out.

My words leave me wondering, clueless
without a doubt.

Him.

Welcome

"Focus on me," he whispers. The words echo in my mind as if my brain were a tunnel. His words linger. They're drawn out with each syllable hesitating to pass his lips. His command trails off, as does his voice. It arose again with, "Follow me."

Similar to his order before, his words were protracted. His pleading engulfed my ability to forgo the demands. My will is feeble; his control robust. He insists, I comply. And to Hell, he leads me.

"Welcome," he hisses with a slur, "...welcome home."

My Killer

Just the thought of him sent me to a world of my own; I liked it.

I could escape my hollow body and explore something unknown. I wasn't where I

needed to be, but I wanted him, and he wanted me.

He knows where to put his hands, and I know what to do with mine.

He acted as if everything would always end up fine.

There was no small talk, only deep endless conversations of our bodies when our lips would lock.

When he looked me in the eye, I felt so -bare, so reviled.

He was the one who stripped me, admiring what he had killed.

You don't catch feelings for your killer, might as well be known as a sin, but I caught feelings for mine as I watched him down a bottle of gin.

Not a trial could prove his guilt.

No matter who took the case,

his devilish touch could easily hide the blood
on my lace.

I'll go back, though, each time for another
taste;

each time knowing all my morals have gone to
waste.

You don't catch feelings for your killer, might
as well be known as a

sin, but I caught feelings for mine as I watched
him down a bottle of gin.

It's hard to say, a few bleeding cuts and a
trim...

Did he really drown me or

did I choose not to swim?

Our poem

I was looked at and saw in such light by him.
The way he thought the sun reflected my
beauty and the mesmerized expression my
smile gave him

shown into me as a feeling of security.

My laugh crashed onto his shores with a wave
of knowing all is right,

and he would await the tide while staring
down the sunset in my eyes.

I knew I drew him in, unlike calm waters.

Willing and loose, he let me drift him out to
sea.

He never felt the need for sunblock or a boat.

He wanted the sunshine to which he
compared to my presence to stain his skin,

as my lips would his cheek–and he wanted to
sink into my waters; a satisfying way to relax.

I, in metaphor, am his vacation. And he, my
only tourist.

Glass

We're two shattered glass panes,

cutting ourselves with each other's pain.

Our memories are foggy from when it was all clear, and now we tip toe in the crystal disputes left here.

Mosaic battles puzzled each of our brains,

only to find out our history is shown through patterned stains.

Windows give a look inside the home, but ours kept it secret with only the curtains shown.

Throwing boulders to crack one another

before we ask the elephant in the room of the answers he smothers.

We streak the same,

yet the filthy fingers ran across us aren't the subject of our blame.

Our frames are designed to fit neatly together,

but our broken pieces dampen the house from the outside weather.

We're grains of sand combined to make the perfect window,

but we're just a broken mirror.

Seasons

I can feel your waves crash onto me like a bank of sand.

Closing my eyes, you whisper soft words into my numb hands.

Your murmurs warm the frostbite away,

for you are the flame kept burning through the chill of the winter, night and day.

They.

Why Did you leave me?

I'm hollow and gone.

You took my soul.

Everything I was, like a thief, you stole.

My days became nights.

Cold, restless, and silent—

I sat in fear of the emptiness you made grow.

Once, when we were whole, you accompanied me.

Together we walked, and together we talked.

You stayed, and I wasn't alone.

With you, I felt a feeling— I had a sense of reality

and maybe an explanation.

Your existence burned slow.

A piece of me left; it went with you.

A part of me I let you borrow. And a part of me you stole.

You.

You're an abyss. You're my cavernous crater.

You're not my shelter. You're not my creator.

You birth my anguish. You silence my
language.

You're always the victor, but you say it's fair.

You strike a match to me.

You set fire to the body in which we share.

You fill my cerebrum with clutter.

You seize my actions and words to a stutter.

Your monosyllabic lyrics echo.

Your sound strident.

You're a seed of misfortune set to grow.

You abuse my physique to gain your fame.

You make me nothing more than a doddering
voice of pain.

You.

Captive

You've built walls around me—

holding me hostage with a key

and a choice to leave, but I stay.

You've starved my brain and taken my
sympathy, leaving my mind nothing but
empty.

You fed me lies, but I gave you your way.

You've caged my poetry

with "intentions" to set it free.

For you, I've forbidden my talent to play.

I know you're my burden,

and I, your fortune.

Spare my life for my devotion.

Store me in abditory,

a place of high value.

Locked in by my own hands.

you hold me captive because I let you.

You are no ghost to see,

just a fragment of imagination fooling me as I know you're in my head.

You've labeled me innocently,

while incriminating me—a justice to serve with dread.

In opinions, your thoughts disagree.

Holding me accountable for our ways to be,

you left me unable to tell them you fled.

I know you're my burden, and I, your fortune.

Spare my life for my devotion.

Store me in abditory,

a place of high value.

Locked in by my own hands,

you hold me captive because I let you.

We

My tragedy, my calamity, the burden upon my conscience—you are the downpour of my aptitude enfranchised by my forecast.

My catastrophe, my misfortune, my personal adversity—you are the manufacturer of iniquitous thoughts in my infamous self-torturing plots.

My tribulation, my misery, my insufferable anguish—you cast a silhouette over my merriment and place a celebratory beacon upon my detriment.

My soul, my body, my mind — you arouse a flame from the burning embers of my pain,

but you are mine. and we are one.

Together we unravel all my knots until I fall undone.

I.

I

I.

I don't feel terrestrial,

I don't feel human.

I don't feel normal.

I feel celestial.

I feel abstract.

I feel eccentric.

I confuse myself when

I look in the mirror.

I see an unidentified reflection.

Who is looking back at me?

Why can't I take this mask off?

What happened to my appearance?

When did I change?

Where did I go?

I am an alien.

I am a stranger.

I am lost.

I can't find myself.

I'm trapped in a body that is not mine.

I'm trapped in a mind that is too much mine.
Everyone says

I look the same, but difference is the only
notice I obtain.

I.

I'm Tired

Drained of vitality, I am eradicated from my youthful

essence. Facile tasks violently liquidate my capability to maintain any ebullience of a valuable living. A tiring

epoch, I am dated in. My actions seize all worth. My endeavor

and energetic attempts have drained my bank of desire. I am a mirage of vigor, shielding my weakness and tire from

onlookers for the sake of my dignity.

I'm tired.

My Mind

My mind is a barren wasteland that no human should have to encounter.

I bury myself. Into a shallow grave, I stand.

A pit of sorrow, I lay upon. I leave my words my thoughts' slave.

My wondering is dragged along with me, its case impermeable, its chauvinism upon my body, deadly.

The faint idea of ever escaping a place called my own, left me drained and lethargic.

It's an action that will never be played gracefully, and will forever remain unknown.

I towel down the damp sky of the city so abandoned where I stay.

Never caring as to who might enter, but endlessly obsessing over what they might say. The sign of a dead

end is where time plays its part. They'll turn back around.

I'll be left alone, abandoned just as the ending glow of a fire's spark.

Catacombs

I am lost in a catacomb of thoughts— a cemetery of my values entombed. I am on the equator of reality and what's in my head. I'm left to scruple, to define my actuality, to pardon my mind's mistakes for convincing me that my mind's

demons are tangible and alive. The brooding of my tenacious illness confines me in melancholia, and I am incarcerated in manic highs alongside of gloomy slopes of desolation, neither with

serenity. I am roaring with suffocating screams; they mark the

amplitude of my disease. My intellect rescues my ignorance of its inability to interpret the verisimilitude of my body's fiends, and I am adrift a sea

of shambles. My captain lost in captivity held by the deficiency of my encephalon. My body is a frame of death. My mind a murderer, and I am its victim.

My Shadow

My shadow never leaves me. It hides itself in the crevasses of my brain. It stays, seeping into my mind drop by drop. Black matter clogs my cerebrum, and all I can see is the devil himself face to face with the being my soul embodies.

He shushes me with his finger on his lip. My mouth is sewn shut by his order. His limits are not tested, for I know he owns by body. He governs my mentality. The city of cells I am formed by obey his commands. He intertwines his fingers with mine to cuff

my hand to his. We're attached, never to be separated. Hell is ecstasy compared to the

feel of his skin draped upon my body like cloth. I wear him as attire. He is my silhouette, and forever he is casted upon my happiness. I am never safe. In the dark, he dances. My vision captured by his merriment upon the walls. In the light, he creeps beneath me, duplicating every movement I make. He stays to taunt me, and I'm never alone, for my shadow never leaves me.

Cureless

I'm cureless;

A lost soul without cause or reason, wandering lonely streets crowded with busy beings;

A hopeless beam of light that's nothing more than the shadow of the moon;

An endless crater from a hollow body longing for celestial help, being no earthly from enough;

A sorrow narrative of a life hardly lived, but cowered within itself as both its safety and fear;

A treacherous cement model left on display for all to view unknowing of its pain and agony, but acknowledged to the smile plastered upon the face of the concrete manikin.

In the end, I'm left untreated. I'm left with death itself the only solution. Research, medication, and science are no match for what devours the thing I am originally and forever trapped in:

myself.

Thief

I was taken.
I was stolen from my body.
I was robbed of a beautiful mind.
My thief is cunning.
Their wickedness led to the infection in my
mind.
Their fingers laced with lies ran themselves
along the strands of my hair, allowing
poisoned words to seep into my skin.
Their eyes the color of sin searched my body
for a place to burrow a sickness of loathsome
torture.
Underneath my brain, the incurable malady
rested, waiting for arousal.
My crook sought after my decomposition.
Hoisting themselves on the lids of my eyes,
awaiting the moment with impatience.
They clung to my body with force and the
ability to control.
My abductor sent waves of incurable madness
through the streams of blood flowing
throughout my body, and I am never to be
saved.
So, I join them, counting down till the last

moments of my remaining sanity.

And just as a grin grows upon the face of guile that has deprived me of a living...I'm gone.

Diagnosis

I can't escape myself. I am trapped in a body with a soul who longs for enfranchisement. My voice is inhibited with restraints placed by my cognitive fiends, and I am unholy - drenched in sin by the Devil himself. He is my brains politician. Wealthy, thieving, and rich with lies, he dictates my cerebrum with rules and regulations placed only to destroy me, as does She.

She purloins my breath, leaving me to suffocate in a predicament caused by her

ability to formulate false, vile accusations against those who reach out to give me their hand.

Together they've made themselves monarchs of my body. My brain is wicked with a disease. My genetic curse has raped me from ever living the habitual lifestyle of my peers. Forever, they will

remain the bane of my body. Forever, I will remain trapped in their territory.

My Music

My body would croon a soprano tune. A drone wouldn't be heard, as it was never to pass my lips, but the subdued vibrations of depression nested in my throat, developing its deepness.

Its octave replacing my light hum. My body now sways to the blues my voice emits through silent sobs and echoing cries for help.

I cannot contain my pain any longer, for my larynx is growing weak with despondency and tire. My song of misery is the theme to which I live by. I am a lyric of

sorrow; my notes, morose. The thoughts I indite are my hymn. now I beg, sing along.

It.

Change

You're never the same. You change, even if you don't realize it. The difference between a second may not be much, but there is a difference. Change may favor you, but disaster is inevitable where there's change. So, let me ask you this: What color is the sky at this exact moment?

I was a smile. I was happy. I was full of life. I was a beam of light shining through a windowpane on Sunday morning, just as the sun had risen. I was the sound of an old record player still in action, humming oldies and echoing throughout the house. I was the coffee cup you cuddled in your

hand while snuggled in a blanket after a long night's rest. I was the laugh that made others laugh. I was the feel of the first day of summer, a day no child could wait patiently for. I was the first shower of spring, inviting and warm. My mouth shown crooked teeth that cued an "aw", and my eyes were glazed with a bright future. My nose sniffled at the pollen floating about, not from crying. My cheeks were sanguine, red like a rose. I was a garden, each

of my flowers unique and vibrant, but my sickness harvested me.

What has taken over me is a monster, a Hitler of an illness. It gives me thoughts, and I take action. I beg, tempting suicide to convey me to another life, one with ease. It gives me a definition to which I'm familiar with, but not in understanding of its power over me. A suffocating cry of agony and doom, I define. It has made me a celestial breath in deep space, one sure to be my last.

It has possessed my mind. My mind is a birth without a death; an immortal mortal; a question without an answer. My mind is the last breath of a sick child; the definition of a bittersweet tragedy. For the juvenal soul, there is no more suffering, just ease, yet it's devastating. That devastation is almost selfish because we don't cry for the child, we cry for ourselves. I'm selfish in a sense as well. I sob at my brain, for it is my bittersweet tragedy. It is the very thing keeping me alive while taking away my ability to be, little by little. And it's working.

It has gripped my body in its hands. My body is now cosmogyral, whirling around the universe in waves of tangible sound: a sickening shriek. My hands disobey me. Pulling my hair and scratching my skin, they mark my sickness onto the epidermis covering the muscles in charge of the harassment. My fingernails are chewed short for my personal safety, for they are weapons. I dodder when I walk—slowly and trembly, I carry myself. I crawl, hand and knee, to my death only to be drug on my spinal column against the earth by life towards the gates of Heaven and Hell and shoved back into my body. The weight of my skin holds me down with an invisible force, seizing my desire to roam about. I strand myself on an island of pity, my body held captive by my mind, and I can't escape. I am now anything but a smile. I've changed. I'm no longer myself, nor am I the shadow of whom my soul embodied. I am a new being. Just as the firmament turns to a deeper shade of itself each second until

its cycle renews the arctic blue it once was, I have changed. To end, let me ask you this: What color is the sky now?

.

It's

It's still there—taunting me in echoes to the brim of my will to push it away and not think.

It grieves my soul with combers of agony and lust for Felo-De-Se.

It has made me abscess on deaths right hand, blistering his skin with my presence.

It has fertilized the growth of knives upon my fingertips so they'll obey and sever my body from the safety it once clung to.

It has made me a villain to my existence.

It has nested beneath my brain long enough, and

It's ready to be in control.

Suicide

I bathe in confusion.

An explanation of unworthiness, distance, and time, my sea.

I drank a cup of poison my own hand poured and delivered to my lips as if destined to be.

I rest my head to a bed of nails, my weakness, my thoughts.

Communication seized, for I know no sea nor destiny do thy murder but the.

Words

My vowels, syllables, and meanings drain onto
a once

clean sheet. A memory of the past, an event
for the future;

you use me to indite your thoughts in the
present as a way of closure.

A clear vacant hole I can fill between lines of
blue or black.

You use me to reassure yourself that what
once left will come back.

Quotes.

I'm wasting away on the inside, yet I birth these words onto you — for my exterior still has breath.

~

I know not of who I am outside this sorrow and unrelenting depression; to

seek serenity and happiness horrifies me without question.

~

I have an abusive relationship with my mind. It devourers my smile and destroys my happiness for my own "protection."

~

My mind is a paradox. It's boisterous, yet ever so calm and still; so very loud, but gracefully

silent. It is the very thing holding me back while pushing me forward.

~

I talk about them like they're still here. Their poisonous whisper still lingers in my ear, but who's to say they're gone?

~

Emptiness is a feeling that swallows all other feelings and digests them into numb torment.

--

They're back. I no longer feel dull, only their presence— such a sweet, sorrow company.

--

I teach others to swim, but I let myself drown.

--

The light in your eyes could brighten the darkest city placed in my dim-lit soul.

--

I profit from my writing—not in gold, but in riches a wealthy man desires.

--

You make me grow, but you're the florist that cuts my stem and steals my leaves to pretty me up and take away life from me.

--

My brain is stagnating due to a medicated mindset and a decomposing sanity.

Thank you.

Author's Note

For anyone suffering with a mental illness: You are not alone, you are not worthless, powerless, or voiceless.

You are valued and important.

I, myself, am diagnosed with an anxiety disorder, schizophrenia, and seasonal depression. I write as a way to cope with the demons who have invaded my mind. Every word I compose is about my personal intangible illnesses.

There is help, and there are ways to defeat the illness that attempts, and sometimes succeeds, to sway your mind.

You are bigger than your body's psychological brute.

Stay safe.

Made in the USA
Middletown, DE
06 March 2018